MW00888507

MEDICAL MATH

Math and My World

Kieran Walsh

Rourke
Publishing LLC
Vero Beach, Florida 32964

www.rourkepublishing.com

PHOTO CREDITS:
Cover photo by Corbis.com. All other photos from AbleStock.com, except for pages 19, 23, 34 by the author and illustration of pill bottle © Getty Images

Technical Advisor: Kurt Konieczny, M.D.

Editor: Frank Sloan

Cover and interior design by Nicola Stratford
Page layout by Heather Scarborough

Library of Congress Cataloging-in-Publication Data

Walsh, Kieran.
  Medical math / by Kieran Walsh.
     p. cm. -- (Math and my world)
Includes bibliographical references and index.
Contents: Life expectancy -- Average height -- Weight -- Body mass index
-- Body temperature -- Blood pressure -- Vision -- Hearing -- Medicine.
  ISBN 1-58952-380-6 (hardcover)
 1. Mathematics--Study and teaching (Elementary)--Juvenile literature.
2. Medicine--Juvenile literature. [1. Mathematics. 2. Medicine. 3.
Body, Human.] I. Title. II. Series: Walsh, Kieran. Math and my world.

  QA135.6.W325 2003
  610'.1'51--dc22

                                    2003011559

Printed in the USA

w/w

TABLE OF CONTENTS

INTRODUCTION

Whether you know it or not, you have probably encountered math in relation to medicine and health many times.

For instance, at some point in your life you may have had a headache, or something worse, like a sprained ankle. Maybe your parents gave you some aspirin to help ease the pain. For aspirin, a standard **dosage**—the amount of medicine an adult should take—is two pills.

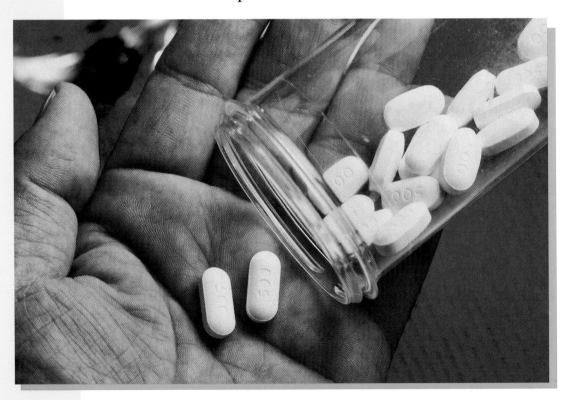

Taking medicine involves some simple math. The dosage, or amount of medicine, is often written somewhere on the outside of a pill.

4

If each pill contains about 500 mg (**milligrams**) of aspirin, how many milligrams of aspirin are you taking with two pills?

You can find out by multiplying:

$$2 \times 500 = 1000$$

1,000 milligrams!

The next time you visit the doctor's office, take a good look around. Numbers are everywhere. By reading this book, you should get a good idea of what all those numbers mean and how you can use math to figure out what numbers are healthy or unhealthy.

Regular visits to your family doctor can keep you healthy and happy. How many times a year do you see your doctor?

LIFE EXPECTANCY

The number of years a person can be expected to live is called his or her **life expectancy**. As of the year 2002, the average life expectancy of a person born in the United States was 77.4 years of age.

You can do some simple math with that number. If you subtract your age from 77.4, the result will give you a rough idea of how much longer you will probably live.

Do you have a little brother or sister? Using math, can you determine how much older you are than they are? Do you know your parents' ages? How much younger are you?

It's only a *rough idea*, though, because that number—77.41—is an **average**. An average is a number that is used to represent a group of numbers. The life spans of millions of different people are used to calculate the average life span of a person.

In fact, 77.41 is not just an average, it is *an average of other averages.* This is because life expectancy varies for different types of people, like people of different sexes and races.

Did you know, for example, that women live slightly longer than men? The life expectancy for women is 80.2 years, while the life expectancy for men is 74.5 years. Can you calculate the average of those two numbers?

If the life expectancy for women is 80.2 years, and the life expectancy for men is 74.5 years, how much longer do women live compared to men?

First, add them up:

$$80.2 + 74.5 = 154.7$$

Then divide the result by the number of **addends**:

$$154.7 \div 2 = 77.35$$

You can round that number up to 77.4—which is the average life expectancy!

People in countries with good health care, clean water, and plenty to eat will generally have a greater life expectancy than people in countries that do not have such resources.

For instance, the people of Andorra, a small country in Europe, have a life expectancy of 83.48 years. How would you compare the lifespan of a typical American with that of a typical Andorran?

You can do this by using subtraction. Just subtract the smaller number from the larger number:

$$83.48 - 77.4 = 6.08$$

So an Andorran lives roughly 6 years longer than an American.

Meanwhile, the people of the Solomon Islands, which are located to the northeast of Australia, have a life expectancy of 71.82 years. To compare that with the life expectancy of an American, just subtract the smaller number from the larger number:

$$77.4 - 71.82 = 5.58$$

A resident of the Solomon Islands lives roughly 6 years *less* than an American.

You can see that, while these numbers vary slightly, they are all roughly in the same range. Just for contrast, though, consider the residents of Botswana, a country in Africa. The life expectancy of a person in Botswana is 35.29 years. How does that figure compare with the life expectancy of an American?

$$77.4 - 35.29 = 42.11$$

The average American lives about 42 years longer than a person living in Botswana.

Dog Years

Even if you don't own a dog, you are probably familiar with the concept that each year of a dog's life is roughly equal to 7 human years. It's actually far more accurate to say that the first 2 years of a dog's life are equal to roughly 10.5 human years; then each dog year after that is equal to about 4 human years.

Using those instructions, how old is a dog of 4 years? You can find out by multiplying, and then adding:

$$2 \times 10.5 = 21 \qquad\qquad 2 \times 4 = 8$$

$$21 + 8 = 29$$

A 4-year-old dog is about 29 human years old!

If this puppy is one month old, about how old would that be in human years?

AVERAGE HEIGHT

Do you know how tall you are? Do you realize that you're probably not done growing yet? That's right. You're going to get bigger and taller!

There's no surefire way of knowing how tall you will be when your body is done growing, but you can get a pretty good idea by referring to *average height*.

Taller people may be better suited to particular sports, like basketball.

Average height is not the same for men as it is for women. The average height for men is roughly 5'10". The correct way of saying that number is *five feet, ten inches*.

The average height for a woman is about 5'5". How would you say that aloud?

Exactly! *Five feet, five inches*.

This is how people typically express height—feet followed by inches. In fact, most people don't even bother saying feet or inches because it's taken for granted that that's the measurement being used. Instead, everyone just states the two numbers.

So now that we've established that you don't need to say feet or inches, how would you express the average height for a man?

Most people would just say, "five, ten."

And how would most people say the average height for women?

"Five, five."

You can also express height *entirely in inches*. To do so, you'll need a little math.

For instance, the average height for men is 5'10". How many inches is that?

There are 12 inches in a foot. You can determine how many inches are in five feet by using multiplication:

$$5 \times 12 = 60$$

There are 60 inches in 5 feet. All you have to do now is add the remaining inches:

$$60 + 10 = 70$$

So the average height for men is about 70 inches.

And what about women? The average height for a woman is 5'5". You already know that there are 60 inches in 5 feet, so you can just add the 5 extra inches:

$$60 + 5 = 65$$

So the average height for women is about 65 inches.

On average, adult men are slightly taller than adult women.

Remember, people don't usually express height in inches. But the conversion of height into inches will become a useful tool when you calculate **Body Mass Index.**

Dwarfism and Gigantism

There are some people who are exceptionally short or exceptionally tall. Human beings between 2 and 4 feet tall are classified as **dwarfs**, while **giants** are classified as being well above 7 feet.

The causes for dwarfism or gigantism can usually be traced to the **pituitary gland**, a portion of the brain that secretes growth hormones. An excess of these hormones can cause gigantism. On the other hand, a malfunction of the pituitary gland can result in the body not getting enough growth hormones, which leads to dwarfism.

Using math, can you compare the heights for dwarfism and gigantism with the average heights given above?

WEIGHT

Weight is a big consideration when determining a person's overall health. Unlike height, though, weight isn't expressed as a fixed number. Instead, weight is typically expressed as a **range,** or group, of numbers.

If you weigh yourself on a regular basis, you will notice that the numbers you get change slightly. You can use these numbers to get an idea of your own average weight. For instance, if your readings for three weeks were 60, 62, and 59, what would your average weight be?

Take a look at this chart:

Weight (Lbs.)

Height	HEALTHY								OVERWEIGHT							OBESE				
4'10"	91	96	100	105	110	115	119	124	129	134	138	143	148	153	158	162	167	172	177	181
4'11"	94	99	104	109	114	119	124	128	133	138	143	148	153	158	163	168	173	178	183	188
5'0"	97	102	107	112	118	123	128	133	138	143	148	153	158	163	168	174	179	184	189	194
5'1"	100	106	111	116	122	127	132	137	143	148	153	158	164	169	174	180	185	190	195	201
5'2"	104	109	115	120	126	131	136	142	147	153	158	164	169	175	180	186	191	196	202	207
5'3"	107	113	118	124	130	135	141	146	152	158	163	169	175	180	186	191	197	203	208	214
5'4"	110	116	122	128	134	140	145	151	157	163	169	174	180	186	192	197	204	209	215	221
5'5"	114	120	126	132	138	144	150	156	162	168	174	180	186	192	198	204	210	216	222	228
5'6"	118	124	130	136	142	148	155	161	167	173	179	186	192	198	204	210	216	223	229	235
5'7"	121	127	134	140	146	153	159	166	172	178	185	191	198	204	211	217	223	230	236	242
5'8"	125	131	138	144	151	158	164	171	177	184	190	197	203	210	216	223	230	236	243	249
5'9"	128	135	142	149	155	162	169	176	182	189	195	203	209	216	223	230	236	243	250	257
5'10"	132	139	146	153	160	167	174	181	188	195	202	209	216	222	229	236	243	250	257	264
5'11"	136	143	150	157	165	172	179	186	193	200	208	215	222	229	236	243	250	257	265	272
6'0"	140	147	154	162	169	177	184	191	199	206	213	221	228	235	242	250	258	265	272	279
6'1"	144	151	159	166	174	182	189	197	204	212	219	227	235	242	250	257	265	272	280	288
6'2"	148	155	163	171	179	186	194	202	210	218	225	233	241	249	256	264	272	280	287	295
6'3"	152	160	168	176	184	192	200	208	216	224	232	240	248	256	264	272	279	287	295	303
6'4"	156	164	172	180	189	197	205	213	221	230	238	246	254	263	271	279	287	295	304	312

*Source: The National Heart, Lung, and Blood Institute

This chart gives a basic idea of whether a person of a particular height has a healthy weight, is overweight, or **obese**. The numbers on the chart apply to both men and women.

For instance, consider a person who is 5'10" tall. Using the numbers on this chart, can you calculate the difference in pounds between a healthy weight for a person of 5'10," and a weight that would categorize that person as obese? What about the difference in pounds for a healthy weight and being overweight?

It's a bit tricky, because with this scale you're not dealing with single numbers. Instead, you're dealing with **series** of numbers. Simply put, a series is a sequence of numbers. For instance, a person of 5'10" could weigh anywhere between 132 and 167 pounds and be considered healthy. A weight between 174 to 202 pounds, though, would be considered overweight. Finally, a weight between 209 to 264 pounds would mean that person is obese.

To simplify the math you'll need to do, you need to find the **medians** of these series. The median is the middle number in a series of numbers.

Although they are not the same things, finding the median of a series of numbers is very much like calculating an average. It is a two-step process involving addition, followed by division.

First of all, find the median for a *healthy* weight. To start, you add the numbers of the series:

$$132 + 139 + 146 + 153 + 160 + 167 = 897$$

Then divide the result by the number of addends, or the numbers that you added:

$$897 \div 6 = 149.5$$

So, the median of a healthy weight for a person of 5'10" is 149.5!

Next, calculate the median of the overweight range:

$$174 + 181 + 188 + 195 + 202 = 940$$
$$940 \div 5 = 188$$

So the median for the overweight range is 188!

Calculate the median for the obese range:

$$209 + 216 + 222 + 229 + 236 + 243 + 250$$
$$+ \ 257 + 264 = 2126$$
$$2126 \div 9 = 236.22$$

Now you have the medians for all three ranges:

Healthy = 149.5

Overweight = 188

Obese = 236.22

What is the difference in pounds between a healthy weight for a person of 5'10" and a weight that would categorize that person as obese? All you need to do now is subtract:

$$236.22 - 149.5 = 86.72$$

The difference between a healthy weight and an obese weight for a person of 5'10" is about 87 pounds!

For a person of the same height, what is the difference in pounds for a healthy weight and being overweight?

$$188 - 149.5 = 38.5$$

The difference is about 39 pounds!

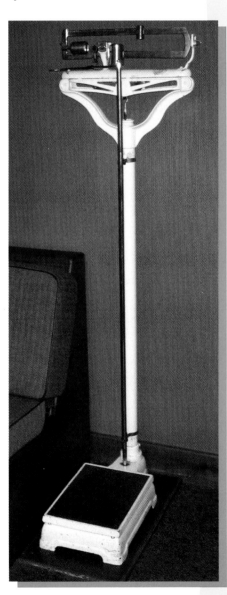

The scales used in a doctor's office, like this one, don't look like the scales you have at home.

BODY MASS INDEX

Your body's ability to do its work depends on your health. If you don't take care of your body, it becomes much more difficult for it to do its work, and that can lead to problems.

Obesity, or the condition of being overweight, is a very serious health problem. Many health risks, including diabetes, high blood pressure, stroke, and arthritis, can result from obesity.

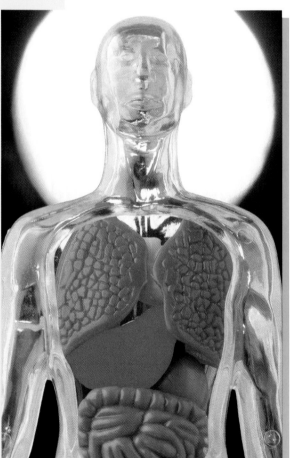

Body Mass Index (BMI) is a simple calculation people can use to gauge obesity. A person's BMI can be determined by dividing his or her weight in pounds by his or her height in inches *squared*, and then multiplying the result by 705. Why 705?

Your body is actually an extremely complex machine. And, like all machines, the body does work. Obesity can make it harder for your body to do this work.

The formula for calculating BMI is actually gauged for the metric system, which is the standard of measurement for most of the world. Multiplying the results by 705 converts to the U.S. Customary System of Measurement.

Before you try any of that math, though, let's talk about **squaring**. If a number in an equation is squared, that means it should be *multiplied by itself.* For instance, the number five squared would look like this in an equation:

$$5^2$$

That little number two to the right of the five is called an **exponent**. The exponent tells you what the *power* of the larger number is. In this case, the number five is to the second power. People usually call the second power squared.

What would 5 squared equal?

$$5 \times 5 = 25$$

5 squared is equal to 25.

The only other exponent to have a nickname (like squared for the second power) is 3, which is called *cubed.* Here, for instance, is how you would write five cubed:

$$5^3$$

And five cubed equals:

$$5 \times 5 \times 5 = 125$$

Bearing all that in mind, what would the equation for Body Mass Index look like?

$$\text{Weight (in Pounds)} \div \text{Height (in Inches)}^2 \times 705$$

Now put that equation to use. Imagine that you're calculating the BMI for a person who weighs 125 pounds and is 5 feet tall. What is his BMI?

First of all, convert the person's height to inches. We know that there are 12 inches in a foot, so:

$$12 \times 5 = 60$$

Our imaginary person is 60 inches tall.

Now let's plug our numbers into the BMI equation:

$$125 \div 60^2 \times 705$$

Now we have to deal with squaring.

What is 60 squared?

$$60 \times 60 = 3600$$

So now what does the equation look like?

$$125 \div 3600 \times 705$$

Just to make things simpler, you can do this in two steps. First, the division:

$$125 \div 3600 = 0.034$$

And then the multiplication:

$$0.034 \times 705 = 24.47$$

So, the Body Mass Index of our imaginary person is 24.47!

But what does that mean?

Generally—very generally—speaking, a Body Mass Index of around 21 is healthiest, while a BMI of 28 or greater indicates a high risk for illness. So, with a BMI of 24.47, our imaginary person is overweight, but not in any great danger.

It is helpful when calculating BMI to remember that the numbers are all relative. In other words, a person with a BMI of 22, say, is somewhat healthier than a person with a BMI of 23, but neither one is perfect. Body Mass Index isn't like a test score—it's just a quick way of determining a person's obesity.

Hydrostatic Weighing and Skinfolds

You may be wondering if the formula for Body Mass Index is only useful for a *general* idea of a person's body fat. What are some more accurate ways to measure body fat?

One of the *most* efficient ways is with **Hydrostatic** weighing. Hydrostatic weighing is done by submerging a person in water and then taking their weight. Fat floats while in water. So, by comparing a person's normal weight with his or her hydrostatic weight, the percentage of body fat can be determined.

Of course, most doctors can't afford to have a giant water tank in their office! That is why they prefer to test fat composition by using calipers. Fat calipers are made to pinch folds of skin. The size of the area being pinched gives a good idea of how much fat there is beneath the skin.

Fat calipers are one of the most convenient ways for doctors to check a patient's body fat content. As you can see, the caliper has a series of numbers on the side that shows a person's fat percentage when pinching a fold of skin.

BODY TEMPERATURE

When was the last time you had your temperature taken?

It's usually something that happens when you're getting sick. Maybe you've had your temperature taken by one of your parents or the family doctor.

But apart from determining whether or not you'll have to go to school, what does a person's body temperature mean? Why is it important?

The thing is, there are two types of animals in the world, cold-blooded and warm-blooded.

Warm-blooded animals include birds ▶
and mammals—animals with hair.

24

The body temperature of a cold-blooded animal changes depending on the temperature outside. This is why you'll sometimes find snakes resting in a patch of sunlight. They need that sun in order to stay warm. Snakes are cold-blooded.

Human beings, though, are warm-blooded animals. In other words, our body temperature remains the same regardless of what the temperature is outside. For human beings, "normal" body temperature is around 98.6 degrees Fahrenheit. Certain illnesses, though, like a fever, will push a person's body temperature up drastically.

What if a person's temperature is 102 degrees Fahrenheit? How many degrees above normal body temperature is that?

$$102 - 98.6 = 3.4$$

So, a temperature of 102 degrees is about 3.4 degrees higher than normal.

At what point, though, does a high body temperature become life threatening? One of the signs of heat stroke, for instance, is a body temperature of 106 degrees or more. How many degrees above normal is that?

$$106 - 98.6 = 7.4$$

A temperature reading of 106 degrees is about 7.4 degrees above normal.

The Hypothalamus

Body temperature changes when we are sick because many illnesses interfere with a region of the brain called the **hypothalamus**. The hypothalamus controls many things, including body temperature. So, when you are sick, your temperature goes up.

And you should keep in mind that, although warm-blooded animals don't depend on the temperature outside in the same way as cold-blooded animals, we are still affected by it. In other words, human beings can stand freezing temperatures for a while, but if subjected to them for too long, they can develop **hypothermia**, which is a fancy way of describing a dangerously low body temperature.

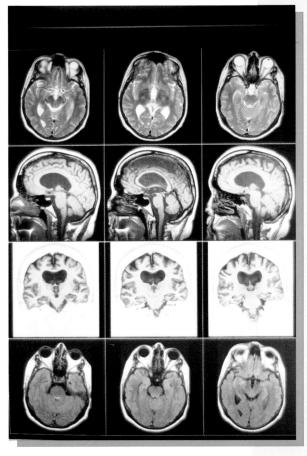

These are X rays of a human brain. The hypothalamus is a small portion of the brain that controls body temperature.

VISION

You already know how important sight is. Without it, you wouldn't be able to read this book.

Some people, though, have poorer sight than others. That is why some people have to wear glasses or contact lenses while other people do not.

Doctors measure sight with an eye chart. You have probably seen one of these during your own eye tests. Most eye charts are made up of ten or eleven lines. Each line is of a group of letters, and each group of letters gets smaller as you go down the chart.

But what does the eye test tell a doctor that helps him or her gauge your vision?

People with less than 20/20 vision may need to wear glasses. ▶

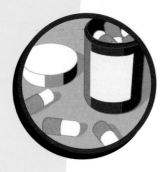

To start with, have you ever noticed that the doctor makes you stand in a particular spot to read the eye chart? To be precise, he makes you stand exactly 20 feet away from the chart—no closer, no farther.

And what about the letters on the eye chart? Why do they start big and then shrink? They do that because they are meant to represent levels of vision. For instance, if you can stand 20 feet from the eye chart and read all the lines, you have perfect vision. Perfect vision is also expressed as twenty twenty, or 20/20 vision.

You've probably noticed that 20/20 is a **fraction**. In a vision fraction, the **numerator** always remains fixed at 20. Can you guess why?

That's right! Because 20 is the number of feet that you are supposed to stand from the eye chart!

The **denominator**, meanwhile, changes according to the level of vision at which you can read.

What if you can't read all the lines on the chart? What if you can only read, say, eight out of ten lines on the chart? In that case, you would have about 20/40 vision.

You can learn something by dividing the fractions for vision. Take 20/20 vision. What would you get if you expressed 20/20 as a percentage?

$$20 \div 20 = 1$$

Twenty divided by twenty equals one. To express this as a percentage, all you have to do is multiply it by 100:

$$1 \text{ x } 100 = 100\%$$

20/20 vision is 100% vision. That makes sense, since 100% is a perfect test score, and 20/20 is considered perfect vision.

20 FOOT
6 METER

20/100
6/30

K H 10

20/80
6/24

D V O 8

20/60
6/18

H V C K

20/50
6/15

Z H V D S 5

20/40
6/12

O C V R K N

20/30
6/9

H O C   R D S 3

20/25
6/7.5

K D V R   Z C O S

20/20
6/6

V R N H Z   D C S K O 2

20/16
6/4.5

Z S V D K   H N O R C

PROFESSIONAL
MODEL
Translucent Eye Cabinet
115 V. AC. 20 WATTS
LISTED 7325

REPLACE
CLEAR LAMP

Let's try some of the same math with 20/40 vision. What would that be expressed as a percentage?

$$20 \div 40 = .5$$
$$.5 \times 100 = 50\%$$

So 20/40 vision is about 50%. In other words, a person with 20/40 vision can see *about half as well* as a person with 20/20 vision. A person with 20/40 vision would probably be prescribed glasses.

What if a person can't even read the top letter, the largest letter on the chart? That would be 20/200 vision. 20/200 is the measure of legal blindness in the United States. Using math, you can see why:

$$20 \div 200 = 0.1$$
$$\times 100 = 10\%$$

A person with 20/200 vision can only see 10 percent of what a person with 20/20 vision sees.

Often, doctors will test both eyes separately. This is done because sometimes a person can have a right eye that measures 20/20, and a left eye that measures 20/30. In a case like that, a person could be described as having one good eye and one bad eye.

◀ *An example of an eye chart. Note that this eye chart has an electrical plug so that it can be lit up.*

You may have had a different type of vision test involving a "screener" like this one.

Screeners

You may have had your eyes tested in a different way—one that didn't involve the use of an eye chart. Perhaps, instead, you were asked to look into a little machine that used slides. That machine was called a vision screener.

In a vision screener, each slide is used to isolate one line of the typical eye chart. The lenses inside the screener, meanwhile, simulate a viewing distance of 20 feet. So, although the technique is slightly different from an eye chart, the numbers used to gauge your eyesight will stay the same.

HEARING

It's more than likely that, if you've had a vision test, you have probably also had a hearing test. They're often done one after the other.

During a hearing test, the doctor makes you wear a pair of headphones. Through the headphones, the doctor plays a sound, or tone. By raising your hand, you indicate whether or not you can hear the tone. With this test, the doctor can determine how good your hearing is. The results of your hearing test are based on your ability to hear tones at different volumes. Volume is the measure of the **intensity** of a sound.

Volume is typically expressed in **decibels**. The word "decibel" actually comes from two words. The second half, "bel," refers to a unit of sound measure that was developed by Alexander Graham Bell, the person who invented the telephone. Meanwhile, the first half, "deci," is a Greek word meaning *one-tenth.* So, a decibel is actually *one-tenth of a bel.*

The symbol for decibel is made of a small "d," and an uppercase "B," like this: "dB."

Here are a few common sounds with their decibel ratings:

Near silence = 0 dB

A whisper = 15 dB

Normal conversation = 60 dB

Lawnmower = 90 dB

Car horn = 110 dB

Jet engine = 120 dB

Firecracker = 140 dB

◀ *The loudness of a whisper is about 15 decibels. How much less is that than the loudness of a firecracker, which is measured at 140 decibels?*

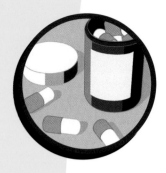

Since you know that a decibel is one-tenth of a bel, how could you find out the number of bels for each of these sounds?

You can find out by using multiplication:

Near silence = 0 dB x 10 = 0 *bels*
A whisper = 15 dB x 10 = 150 *bels*
Normal conversation = 60 dB x 10 = 600 *bels*
Lawnmower = 90 dB x 10 = 900 *bels*
Car horn = 110 dB x 10 = 1100 *bels*
Jet engine = 120 dB x 10 = 1200 *bels*
Firecracker = 140 dB x 10 = 1400 *bels*

As you can see, the louder sounds yield some pretty big numbers. That is why it is easer to refer to sounds in terms of decibels.

Unlike, say, pounds or inches, decibels are not really a unit of measure. Actually, decibels are units of comparison. Using decibels, you can compare the sounds in this list.

How much louder, for instance, is a lawnmower compared to a whisper? To find out, all you have to do is use subtraction:

$$90 - 15 = 75$$

A lawnmower is *75 times* louder than a whisper.

The thing is, the range of sound is very broad. In fact, human beings can only hear a bit of that range.

Take, for instance, near silence, which is about 0 dB. This is about where human beings can begin to hear. That is why 0 dB is thought of as the *threshold of hearing*. Meanwhile, a jet engine, which has a rating of 120 dB, is almost at the *threshold of pain*. The threshold of pain is at 130 dB. This is where the sound is so intense that it actually becomes painful.

Prolonged exposure to very loud sounds can permanently damage your hearing. This is why people who work in construction often wear protective headphones.

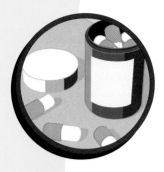

Prolonged exposure to loud noises can damage your hearing. That's why you should be especially careful about using excessive volume when listening to music through headphones.

CONCLUSION

As you get older, you will start to notice that the number of doctors in your life seems to multiply!

As you learned before, the body is like a machine—not just in the sense that it does work—but also in the sense that it is made up of several different parts.

Doctors who focus on the treatment and care of a particular part of the body are known as specialists. There are many different kinds of specialists, including:

Podiatrists – who care for the feet

Optometrists – who care for the eyes

Gastroenterologists – who care for the stomach

In fact, even the dentist is a doctor who specializes in treating and caring for your teeth!

Someday, when you get old enough to have your own children, you will take them to a pediatrician.

And maybe when they're old enough to understand, you can show them all the math involved with medicine!

THE METRIC SYSTEM

We actually have two systems of weights and measure in the United States. Quarts, pints, gallons, ounces, and pounds are all units of the U.S. Customary System, also known as the English System.

The other system of measurement, and the only one sanctioned by the United States Government, is the metric system, which is also known as the International System of Units. French scientists developed the metric system in the 1790s.

The metric system is actually used regularly for some aspects of medicine. As you have seen, dosages are routinely measured in milligrams, and even the formula for Body Mass Index is performed in metric units.

One instance where the metric system does apply to medicine is in regard to body temperature. When measuring temperature, most of the world does not use the Fahrenheit system. Instead, they rely on the Celsius Scale, which treats the freezing point of water as 0° and the boiling point as 100°.

◄ *A pediatrician is a doctor who specializes in the treatment of infants and young children.*

Converting a Fahrenheit reading to a Celsius reading is quite simple. Just subtract 32 from the Fahrenheit temperature and then divide the result by 1.8.

What if you had a temperature of 97°? What is that on the Celsius scale?

$$97 - 32 = 65$$
$$65 \div 1.8 = 36.1$$

Your temperature would be about 36.1° Celsius!

Another instance where the metric system should be taken into account is with vision. In the United States, perfect 20/20 vision is an expression of what a person can see at a distance of 20 feet. In the metric system though, vision would be measured with meters—one meter being equal to about 3.2 feet.

What would 20/20 vision be in the metric system? You can find out with division:

$$20 \div 3.2 = 6.25$$

You can round that number down to 6, which leaves you with a measure of 6/6 for perfect vision!

As you can see, the metric system is pretty easy once you get the hang of it. For practice, you could go through this book and convert some of the numbers to metric.

Try it!

GLOSSARY

addends – the numbers to be combined in an
  addition problem

average – a number used to represent a group of numbers

body mass index – a rough idea of how much fat you
  have on your body

decibels – a measurement of sound

denominator – the bottom number of a fraction

dosage – the amount of medicine instructed by a doctor
  or on the instructions for the medicine

dwarfs – people who measure between 2 and 4 feet tall

exponent – a number that indicates what power to raise
  another number to

fraction – another way of writing a division problem; a
  number composed of two numbers

giants – people who measure 7 feet tall or more

hydrostatic – under water

hypothalamus – a portion of the brain that regulates body temperature

hypothermia – dangerously low body temperature

intensity – force; power

life expectancy – the number of years a person can be expected to live

medians – the middle number of a series

milligrams – a very small unit of measure; one thousandth of a gram

numerator – the top number of a fraction

obese – dangerously overweight

pituitary gland – a portion of the brain that regulates growth

range – a group of numbers

series – a sequence of numbers, usually in order

squaring – multiplying a number by itself

Further Reading

Zeman, Anne and Kate Kelly. *Everything You Need To Know About Math Homework*. Scholastic, 1994.

Websites to Visit

http://www.halls.md/body-mass-index/bmirefs.htm
Formula for Body Mass Index

http://www.biorap.org/br8factsaround.html
BioRap – Life Expectancy Around the World

http://www.howstuffworks.com/question124.htm
How Stuff Works – What is a Decibel?

http://www.nhlbi.nih.gov/
National Heart, Lung, and Blood Institute

http://www.hhs.gov/
United States Department of Health and Human Services

INDEX

About the Author

Kieran Walsh has written a variety of children's nonfiction books, primarily on historical and social studies topics, including the recent Rourke series *Holiday Celebrations* and *Countries In the News*. He divides his time between upstate New York and New York City.